The Trial and Ex

For Petit Treason, of Mark and Phillis, Slaves of Capt. John Codman

Who Murdered Their Master at Charlestown, Mass., in 1755; for Which the Man Was Hanged and Gibbeted, and the Woman Was Burned to Death. Including, Also, Some Account of Other Punishments by Burning in Massachusetts

Abner Cheney Goodell

Alpha Editions

This edition published in 2024

ISBN : 9789362095596

Design and Setting By
Alpha Editions
www.alphaedis.com
Email - info@alphaedis.com

As per information held with us this book is in Public Domain.
This book is a reproduction of an important historical work. Alpha Editions uses the best technology to reproduce historical work in the same manner it was first published to preserve its original nature. Any marks or number seen are left intentionally to preserve its true form.

THE TRIAL AND EXECUTION

OF

MARK AND PHILLIS,

IN 1755.

[The following pages are, with slight changes, a reprint from the Proceedings of the Massachusetts Historical Society, of a paper read before that Society, March 8, 1883, in answer to a question propounded at a previous meeting, relative to the authenticity of the tradition that a woman was burned to death in Massachusetts in the year 1755. As this case is the only known instance of the infliction of the common-law penalty for petit treason, in New England, and is not known to have been elsewhere reported, the printers have, at the author's request, struck off, in pamphlet form, a limited number of impressions for the use of persons interested in the history of our criminal jurisprudence, who may not have convenient access to the serial from which it is taken, or who may desire to preserve it separately.]

It is not surprising that the execution of a woman, by burning, so lately as when Shirley was governor,—a period when the province had greatly advanced in culture and refinement,—should seem to any one incredible. Indeed, even so critical and thorough a student of our provincial history as our late distinguished associate, Dr. Palfrey, once wrote to me inquiring if the rumor of such a proceeding had any foundation in fact, and if so, whether the execution took place according to law, or by the impulse of an infuriated mob. It gave me great satisfaction to be able to settle his doubts on this subject by referring him to the records of the Superior Court of Judicature, where the judgment, from which I shall presently read to you, and a copy of which I sent to him, appears at length.

The subject is important at this day only as serving to define the nature of the "cruel and unusual punishments" prohibited by the thirty-first article of the Declaration of Rights, in our state Constitution, since this mode of punishment, having continued after the adoption of the Constitution, cannot have been considered by the framers of that instrument either as "cruel" or "unusual" in the sense in which they used these words.

The particulars of the crime for which the malefactors, Mark and Phillis, were executed are briefly as follows: Captain John Codman, a thrifty saddler, sea-captain, and merchant, of Charlestown, was the owner of several slaves whom he employed either as mechanics, common laborers, or house servants. Three of the most trusted of these, Mark, Phillis, and Phebe,—particularly Mark,—found the rigid discipline of their master unendurable, and, after setting fire to his workshop some six years before, hoping by the destruction of this building to so embarrass him that he would be obliged to sell them, they, in the year 1755, conspired to gain their end by poisoning him to death.

In this confederacy some five or six negroes belonging to other owners were more or less directly implicated. Mark, the leader, was able to read, and signed his examination, hereafter referred to, in a bold, legible hand. He professed to have read the Bible through, in order to find if, in any way, his master could be killed without inducing guilt, and had come to the conclusion that according to Scripture no sin would be committed if the act could be accomplished without bloodshed. It seems, moreover, to have been commonly believed by the negroes that a Mr. Salmon had been poisoned to death by one of his slaves, without discovery of the crime. So, application was made by Mark, first to Kerr, the servant of Dr. John Gibbons, and then to Robin, the servant of Dr. Wm. Clarke, at the North End of Boston, for poison from their masters' apothecary stores, which was to be administered by the two women.

Essex, the servant of Thomas Powers, had also furnished Mark with a quantity of "black lead" for the same purpose. This was, unquestionably, not the harmless plumbago to which that name is now usually given, but galena, or *plumbum nigrum*, a native sulphuret of lead, probably used for a glaze by the potters of Charlestown.

Kerr declined to have any hand in the business; but Robin twice obtained and delivered to Mark a quantity of arsenic, of which the women, Phebe and Phillis, made a solution which they kept secreted in a vial, and from time to time mixed with the water-gruel and sago which they sometimes gave directly to their victim to eat, and at other times prepared to be innocently administered to him by one of his daughters. They also mixed with his food some of the "black lead," which Phillis seems to have thought was the efficient poison, though it appeared from the testimony that he was killed by the arsenic.

The crime was promptly traced home to the conspirators; and on the second day of July, the day after Captain Codman's death, a coroner's jury found that he died from poison feloniously procured and administered by Mark. Ten days later, Quaco,—the nominal husband of Phebe, and one of the negroes implicated,—who was the servant of Mr. James Dalton, of Boston, was examined before William Stoddard, a justice of the peace, and on the same day Robin was arrested and committed to jail. The examination of Quaco was followed by the examination of Mark, and of Phillis, later in the month. These last were taken before the Attorney-General and Mr. Thaddeus Mason.

At the term of the "Superiour Court of Judicature, Court of Assize, and General Goal Delivery," held at Cambridge on the second Tuesday of August following, the grand jury found a true bill for petit treason against Phillis, and against Mark and Robin as accessories before the fact. As this is the only indictment for this offence known to have been found in Massachusetts, and was drawn by that eminent lawyer, Edmund Trowbridge, then Attorney-General, it is worthy of being preserved in print, in connection with the coroner's verdict and the examinations of the suspected parties, which are as follows:—

[Coroner's Inquest.]

[Two-penny stamp.]MIDDLESEX ss.

An Inquisition Indented, Taken at Charlestown Within the County of Middlesex Aforesaid the Second day of July in the Twenty ninth year of the Reign of our Lord George the Second by the Grace of God, of Great Britain France and Ireland, King Defender of the Faith &c., before John Remington Gentleman one of the Coroners of our said Lord the King, Within the County of Middlesex Aforesaid; upon view of the Body of John Codman of Charlestown Aforesaid Gentleman then and there Being dead by the oaths of Josiah Whitemore, Samuel Larkin, Samuel Larkin Junr. Richard Deavens, William Thompson, Nathaniel Brown, Samuel Kettle, John Larkin, Thomas Larkin, David Cheever, Barnabas Davis, Edward Goodwin, Benjamin Brazier, Samuel Sprague, Richard Phillips, Samuel Hendley and Michael Brigden Good and Lawfull men of Charlestown Aforesaid Within the County Aforesaid; Who being Charg'd and Sworn to Inquire for our said Lord the King, When, and by What means, and how the Said John Codman Came to his Death—upon their Oaths do Say that the said John Codman Came to his death By Poison Procured by his negro man servant Mark Which he took and Languishd untill the first of July Current and then died and so the Jurors Aforesaid upon their oaths do Say, that Aforesaid Mark in manner and Form Aforesaid, the Aforesaid John Codman then and there feloniously did Poison against the peace of our Soverign Lord the King his Crown and Dignity—

In Witness, Whereof, as Well I the Coroner Aforesaid, as the Jurors Aforesaid, to this Inquisition have Interchangeably put our hands and Seals, the day And year Abovesaid.

		JOHN REMINGTON *Coroner*	[Seal.]
RICHD PHILLIPS	[Seal.]	JOSIAH WHITTEMORE	[Seal.]
SAMLL KETTELL	[Seal.]	SAML HENDLY	[Seal.]
JOHN LARKIN	[Seal.]	MICHLL BRIGDEN	[Seal.]
SAMUEL LARKIN JNR.	[Seal.]	NATHLL BROWN	[Seal.]
WILLIAM THOMPSON	[Seal.]	DAVID CHEEVER	[Seal.]
THOMAS LARKIN	[Seal.]	SAMLL LARKIN	[Seal.]
RICHARD DEVENS	[Seal.]	BENJAMIN BRAZIER	[Seal.]
		BARNABAS DAVIS	[Seal.]
		SAMUELL SPRAGUE	[Seal.]
		EDWD. GOODWIN	[Seal.]

[Examination of Quaco.]

On the 12th July 1755, was Examined Quacoe a Negro man belonging to Mr James Dalton of Boston Victualler He sd Quacoe says that some time the last winter one Kerr a Negro man belonging to Doctr. Jno Gibbons came to the sd Quacoe & told him that Mark belongg. to Mr Codman had Been wth. him to get some Poyson and the sd. Quaco says that Ker told him that Mark asked the sd. Kerr whither Phœbe had been wth. him for said Poyson. The said Quacoe also says that he Spoke to Phœbe Mr Codman's negro woman whom he called his Wife & told her not to be Concerned with Mark for that she would be Brought into Trouble by him, for that Mark had been wth. Kerr Gibbons to get Poyson, & had askt sd Kerr whither Phœbe had not been wth him for sd Poyson. The sd Quacoe also says that the above discourse wth Phœbe was when they were going to Bed the Saturday night after the discourse had wth. Kerr Gibbons. He also says that he charged her not to be concerned wth. Mark about Poyson on any accot. whatever.

The above Examination Taken on the 12th. July 1755 at Boston

WM STODDARD *J Pacis*

[Mittimus against Robin.]

SUFFOLK ss:

To The Keeper of His Majestys Goal in Boston and to the Constables of Boston Greeting—

L.S.

I herewith Comit to you Mr. Constable Pattin the Body of Robin a Negro man belonging to Dr. William Clarke of the North End of Boston, who is this day Charged wth being Concerned in the Poysoning of the late Mr. John Codman of Charles Town Deceased. Take Care of him and deliver him to The Keeper of His Majestys Goal in Boston; and you the sd Keeper are hereby Commanded to Receive the Body of the Said Robin and him Safely Keep untill he shall be discharged by Due Course of Law,

Given under my hand and Seal at Boston the Twelfth day of July anno Domini 1755 and in the Twenty ninth Year of the Kings Reign.

WM. STODDARD, *Just: Pacis*.

[Examination of Phillis.]

MIDDX ss:

The Examination of Phillis a negro Servant of John Codman late of Charlstown deceased taken by Edmund Trowbridge and Thaddeus Mason Esqrs at Cambridge in the County of Middlesex the 26th. Day of July Anno Domini 1755. And ye 2d of Augt. following—

Questn. Was Mr. John Codman late of Charlstown de[=c]d, your Master?

Answr. Yes he was.

Quest. How long was you his servant?

Answr. He my said Master bought me when I was a little girl and I continued his servant untill his Death.

Questn. Do you know of what sickness your said master died?

Answer. I suppose he was poisoned.

Quest. Do you know he was poisoned?

Answr. I do know he was poisoned.

Quest. What was he poisoned with?

Answr.—It was with that black lead.

Quest. what black Lead is it you mean?

Answr. The Potter's Lead.

Quest. How do you know your sd. master was poisoned with that Lead?

Answr. Mark got some of the said Potter's Lead from Essex Powers and my young mistress Molly found some of the same Lead in the Porringer that my Master's Sagoe was in, he complain'd it was gritty; and that made Miss Molly look into the Porringer, and finding the Lead there, she ask'd me what it was, I told her I did not know.—I cleaned the Skillet the Sagoe was boiled in and found some of the same stuff in the bottom of the skillet that was in the bottom of the Porringer. And presently after Mark was carried to Goal, Tom brought a Paper of the Potter's Lead out of the Blacksmith's Shop, which he said he found there; and I saw it and am sure it was the same with that which Was in the bottom of the Porringer and the Skillet.

Quest. Do you know that any other Poison besides the Potter's Lead was given to your sd master?

Answr. Yes.

Quest. What was it?

Answr. It was Water which was poured out of a Vial.

Quest. How do you know that, that Water was Poison?

Answr. There was a White Powder in the Vial, which Sunk to the Bottom of it.—

Quest. Do you know who put the Powder into the Vial?

Answr. I put the first Powder in.

Quest. Where did you get that Powder?

Answr. Phebe gave it to me up in the Garret, the Sabbath Day morning before the last Sacrament before my master dyed, and Phœbe at the same time told me Mark gave it to her.

Quest. What was the Powder in when Phœbe gave it you?

Answer. It was in a White Paper, folded up Square, both ends being turn'd up, & it was tyed with some Twine.

Quest. How much Powder was there in the Paper?

Answr. There was a good deal of it I believe near an ounce.

Quest. Did you put all that Powder into the Vial?

Answr. No, I put in but a little of it, only so much as lay on the Point of a narrow Piece of flat Iron, with which I put it in, which Iron Mark made & gave it to me to give to Phebe, Mark gave me the sd Iron the Saturday before the Sabbath aforesd. I ask'd him what it was for, he would not tell me; he said Robbin gave him one, and he had lost it; and that he himself went into the shop and made this. I gave the sd Iron to Phœbe that same afternoon, in the Kitchen; and the next morning she gave it to me in the Garret, and Quaco was there with her; she whisper'd to me and told me to take the Paper of Powder which was in the hollow over the Window, and the flat Iron which was with it and put some of it into the Vial with the Iron which I did; and she bid me put some water into it, but I did not; but she afterwards put some in herself, as she told me, and she put it into the Closet in the Kitchen in a Corner behind a black Jug; and the same Vial was kept there untill my master dyed.

Quest. Had your Master any of that Water which was put into the said Vial given to him?

Answr. Yes he had.

Quest. How was it given to him?

Answr. It was poured into his barly Drink and into his Infusion, and into his Chocalate, and into his Watergruel.

Quest. Who poured the Water out of the sd Vial into the Chocalate?

Answr. Phœbe did, and Master afterwards eat it.

Quest. Who pour'd it into his barly Drink?

Answr. I did it myself; I pour'd a drop out of the Vial into the barly Drink, & I felt ugly, and pour'd the Water out of the mug again off from the Barly, and put clean Water into the mug again & cover'd it over that it might boil quick.

Quest. Who pour'd the Water out of the Vial into the Infusion?

Answr. Phœbe did.

Quest. How do you know it?

Answr. I came into the Kitchen and saw her do it.

Quest. Did your master drink the Infusion after that water was so pour'd in?

Answr. He drank one Tea Cup full of it.

Quest. How do you know that Phœbe poured any of the poisoned Water out of the Vial into your Master's Chocalate?

Answr. She told me she had done it.

Quest. When did she tell you so?

Answr. That Same Day.

Quest. Was it before or after your Master eat that Chocalate that the poison'd Water was pour'd into, that She told you so?

Answr. Before he eat it.

Quest. Did you see him eat that Chocalate?

Answr. Yes, I did, he eat it in the Kitchen on a little round Table.

Quest. Who put the Second Powder into the Vial?

Answr. Phœbe put it in; I left Part of the Powder she gave me in the Paper, and she afterwards put that into the Vial as she told me. as I was in the cellar drawing some Cyder, I heard Phœbe tell Mark that the Powder was all out, and all used up;

Quest. When was it that you heard Phœbe tell Mark so?

Answr. The Wednesday before my master dyed.

Quest. Do you know of any more Powder being got to give to your master?

Answer. Yes, but master never took any of it.

Quest. Who got this last Powder?

Answr. Mark got it.

Quest. What did he do with it?

Answr. He gave it to me; in our little House.

Quest. What Sort of Powder was it that Mark gave You?

Answr. I[t?] was white the same as the first.

Quest. What was it in?

Answr. In a Peice of Paper; he had more of that Powder than he gave me, it was in a Paper folded up in a long Square, he tore off Part of that Paper, and put Some of the Powder into it, and gave it to me and kept the rest himself. and at the same time that he gave it to me he told me that Robbin said we were damn'd Fools we had not given Master that first Powder at two Doses, for it wou'd have killed him, and no Body would have known who hurt him, for it was enough to kill the strongest man living; upon which I ask'd Mark how he knew, it would not have been found out, he said that Mr. Salmon's

Negros poison'd him, and were never found out, but had got good masters, & so might we.

Quest. What did you do with that Powder which Mark gave you?

Answr. I put it into the Vial, & set it in the Same Place it was in before, there was some of the first Powder & Water remaining in the Vial when I put this last in.

Quest. Do you know that any of the Water that was in the Vial after you put this last Powder in was given to your Master?

Answr. No, he never had a drop of it. The next Day after Master died Mark came into the Closet where I was eating my Dinner and ask'd me for that Bottle. I ask'd him what he wanted it for, and he would not tell me, but insisted upon having it, upon which I told him that it was there behind the Jugg, and he took it and went directly down to the Shop in the yard, and I never saw it afterwards 'till Justice Mason shew it to me, on the Fast Day night.

Quest. Do you know where Mark got that Powder which he gave to you?

Answr. He had it of Robbin, Doctr Clark's Negro; that liv'd with Mr. Vassall.

Quest. How do you know that Mark had that Powder of Robbin?

Answr. The Thursday night before my master died Mark told me he was going over to Boston to Robbin to get some more Powder for he sd: Phœbe told him yt the other was all out; and Mark went over to Boston, and return'd again about nine o'Clock; and I ask'd Mark if he had got it, and he told me no, he had not, but Robbin was to bring it over the next night; and between 8 & 9 o'Clock that next night, a negro Fellow came to me in our Yard & ask'd me for Mark, And I ask'd him his name but he would not tell me, and I said to him, Countryman, if you'l tell me your name I'll call Mark, for I know where he is, but he would not, I then askt him if he was not Robbin Vassall, (for I mistrusted it was he) and upon that he laughed and said his name was not Robbin Vassall, but he came out of the Country and wanted to see Mark very much about his Child; and upon my refusing to tell him where Mark was the negro went away down to the Ferry, and I followed him at some distance & saw him go into the Ferry Boat, and the Boat put off, with him in it. That same Fryday, in the afternoon, Mark told me, if any Negro Fellow shou'd come; & say that he came out of the Country to call him, I ask'd him what negro it was that he expected wou'd come; he told me it was Robbin, and that he was to say that he came out of the Country to speak with Mark about his Child, and bid me tell no Body about it.

Quest. Do you know Robbin Doctr. Clark's negro?

Answr. I do, and have known him for many years.

Quest. How then happen'd it that you cou'd not certainly tell whether the negro aforesd. that askt for Mark was Robbin or not?

Answr. Because it was dark, So dark I cou'd not see his Face so as certainly to know him, but I am fully satisfyed it was Robbin.

Quest. What Reason have you to be satisfyed it was Robbin?

Answr. That same night I told Mark that a negro Fellow had been there and ask'd for him & wanted him, he ask'd me why I did not call him, I told him our Folks called me and I could not, Mark told me he was very Sorry I did not, and asked me if he gave me any Thing, I told him he did not, he said he was very sorry he did not; then I ask'd him who it was, and he said it was Robbin, and then he told me that he thought Robbin & he had been playing blind-mans Buff, for they had been over the Ferry twice that night and mist one another; and that Elijh Phipps & Timo Rand told him that a negro Fellow had been over the Ferry to speak with him about his Child. And then Mark told me he would the next Night go over to Robbin and get some more of the same Powder, and would bring it over on the Sabbath Day, & he went to Boston on the Saturday night, but did not return till Monday morning, when he brought it and gave it to me in the little House, as I told you before.

Quest. Did you see Robbin at Charlstown in the Time of your master's sickness or about the Time of his Death?

Answr. Yes, I saw him on ye Tuesday the Ship was launched, when my master catch'd Mark buying Drink at Mrs Shearman's to treat him with, & drove him away; and I saw him at Charlstown on the Saturday after my Master was buried; but I did not speak with him at either of those Times. The Tuesday he was before our Shop Door, in the Street, with Mark and had a Bag upon his shoulder; and on the Saturday in the afternoon I saw him going up the Street by our House, while Phœbe and I were washing in the back yard; I told Phœbe there was Robbin a going along this minit, and she said is he? and ask'd me what Cloaths he had on; I told her he had a bluish Coat on lined with a straw coloured or yellow lining and the Cuffs open & lined with the said Yellow lining, and that he had a black wigg on; and I told Phœbe I believed he was gone up to Mark to tell him not to own that he had given any Thing to him, and Phœbe said she believed so to; and I went into the street to the Pump with a Pail to get some Water, designing to see whether he went that Way, and I saw him go right up the main street, and I could see him as far up as Mr. Eleazer Phillips's, and I did not see him afterwards. I never see him with a Wigg on before, but as he went by us he look'd me full in the Face and I knew it was Robbin. When I told Phœbe that Robbin was going by, I thought she saw him, but she questioned whether it was he, and

I told her I was sure it was he, for I had known him ever since he was a boy, and I told her I would lay a mug of Flip that it was he, but she wou'd not; and then it was that I told her I believed he was gone up to Mark &c.

Quest. Do you know what Powder that was which Mark & Phœbe gave you, and you put into the Vial?

Answr. Mark told me it was Ratsbane, but I told Phœbe I believed Mark lied & that it was only burnt allom, for I told her, that upon taking Ratsbane they would directly swell, and Master did not swell; and she said she believed so to.

Quest. How many Times was any of that Water, which was in the Vial aforesd., put into your master's victuals?

Answr. Not above Seven Times.

Quest. When was the first Time?

Answr. The next Monday morning after Phœbe gave me the first Powder. then it was put into his Chocalate, by Phœbe. The next was also put in to his Chocalate by Phœbe on the next Wednesday morning, and I thinking she put in more than she should, told her her hand was heavy, and there was no more put in, that, I know of till the next Fryday, when Phœbe put some into his Chocalate, and my Master eat the Chocalate all the three times aforesaid in the Kitchen, and I was there & saw him; The next was on the Saturday following, when I put Some into his Watergruel, but I felt ugly and threw it away, and made some fresh, and did not put any into that. The next was on the afternoon of the same Saturday, I made him some more Watergruel & pour'd some of the Water out of the Vial into it, and it turned yellow, and Miss Betty, ask'd me what was the matter with the Watergruel and I gave her no answer; but that was thrown away, and more fresh made, and Miss Molly was going to put the same Plumbs in again, and Phœbe told her not to do it, but she had better put in some fresh Plumbs, and she did; and no Poison was put into that; It was by Phœbe's advice that I put it into the first this afternoon. And he had no more, that I know of 'till the next Monday night, when Mark put some of the Potter's Lead into Masters Sagoe.

Quest. How do you know that Mark put any of the Potter's Lead into the Sagoe?

Answer. When I went out of the Kitchen I left the Sagoe in the little Iron Skillet on the Fire, and no body was in the Kitchen then, but when I returned, Mark was Sitting on a Form in the Corner, and I afterwards found Some of that Lead in the Skillet, and neither Phœbe nor I had any Such Lead.

Quest. Do you know of any other Poison prepar'd for, or given to your Master?

Answr. No, I do not.

Quest. Who was it that first contrived the poisoning your Master Codman?

Answr. It was Mark who first contrived it, He told Phœbe and I that he had read the Bible through, and that it was no Sin to kill him if they did not lay violent Hands on him So as to shed Blood, by sticking or stabbing or cutting his Throat.

Quest. When was it that Mark first proposed the poisoning his Master?

Answr. Some time last Winter; he proposed it to Phœbe and I, but we would not agree to it, and told him No Such Thing should be done in the House; This before my Master brought him home from Boston.

Quest. Did he ever afterwards propose the poisoning his sd Master?

Answr. Yes he did, a Week or a Fortnight after my Master brought him home from Boston, he proposed it to me first, and I would not agree to it, and then he proposed it to Phœbe.

Quet. What Reason did Mark give for poisoning his Master?

Answ. He said he was uneasy and wanted to have another Master, and he was concerned for Phœbe and I too.

Quest. Do you know how your Master's Work house that was burnt down came on Fire?

Answr. Yes I do.

Quest. How came it on fire?

Answr. I set it on fire, but it was thro' Mark's means, he gave me no rest 'till I did it.

Quest. How did you Set your Master's Work House on fire?

Answr. I threw a Coal of Fire into some Shavings between the Blacksmith's Shop & the Work House, and I went away & did not see it kindle.

Quest. Who put the Shavings there?

Answr. Mark did.

Quest. Was any Body concern'd in the burning the Work house besides Mark and you?

Answr. Yes, Phœbe knew about it as well as I.

Quest. Where was Phœbe & Mark when you put the Coal of Fire into the Shavings?

Answr. The were up Garret in bed.

Quest. Who first proposed the Setting the Workhouse on fire? and what reason was given for doing it?

Answr. Mark first proposed it, to Phœbe and I; and the Reason he gave us was that he wanted to get to Boston, and if all was burnt down, he did not know what Master could do without selling us.

Quest. Why did you, when Phœbe pour'd Some of the Water out of the Vial into the Chocolate tell her, "her hand was heavy?"

Answr. I thought she pour'd in too much, more than she should I felt ugly and I wan't willing she shou'd put in so much and that he should be kill'd so quick. Mark's orders were to give it in two Doses, that was the Directions Robbin gave to Mark, as Mark told me, and Mark Said Robbin told him there was no more taste in it than in Cold Water.

Quest. Why did you not tell your Master or some of the Family that Phœbe had poisoned the Chocalate, and thereby prevent your Master's eating it?

Answr. I do not know why I did not tell.

The mark of **X** Phillis.

[Examination of Mark.]

MIDDLESEX ss:

The Examination of Mark a Negro Servant of John Codman late of Charlstown deceased taken by Edmund Trowbridge & Thaddeus Mason Esqrs. at Charlstown in the County of Middlesex the ——— Day of July Anno Dom: 1755.

Quest. What is your name?

Answr. Mark.

Quest. Are you a Servant or Freeman?

Answr. A Servant. Mr. John Codman decd: was my master.

Quest. How long was you his Servant?

Answr. For several Years before & untill his Death.

Quest. Do you know what occasion'd your sd. Master's Death?

Answr. He was poisoned.

Q. What was he poisoned with?

A. With Poison that came from the Doctor's.

Q. What Doctor?

Answr. Doctr. Clark that lives at the North End of Boston.

Q. What sort of Poison was that?

A. It was a White Powder put up in a Paper.

Q. How do you know that that Powder came from Doctr. Clark's?

A. Robbin the Negro Fellow that belongs to Doctr. Clark gave it to me.

Q. When & where did Robbin give you that Powder?

An. A Week Day night, at his Master's Barn.

Qu. Was there any Person present with you when Robbin gave you that Powder?

An. No. The first Time, the negro man his fellow Servant called him out, it was in the Evening near 9 o'Clock.

Qu. How many Times had you such Powder of Robbin?

An. Twice only.

Qu. When was the last Time you had any such Powder of him?

An. The Sabbath Day night before my sd. Master died, in the Evening after Candle Light.

Qu. Where was it you had this last Powder of him, and what was it in?

An. He gave it to me in the same Barn, it was done up in a long square in two Papers, the outtermost Paper was brown and the inermost Paper was White, as the other was.

Qu. What did Robbin give you these Powders for?

An. To kill three Pigs belonging to Quaco as Phœbe told me.

Qu. How long ago was it Since Robbin gave you the first of these Powders?

An. I can't certainly tell.

Qu. Was it before Robbin & you were together at John Harris ye Potters Work house?

Ansr. I think it was before.

Qu. How long before was it?

Ansr. About a Week before.

Qu. Did you pay Robbin any Thing for these Powders?

An. No. I did not.

Q. What did you do with them?

Ans. Phœbe had the first; and she sent Phillis for the second and I gave it to her.

Qu. When & where did you give Phœbe the first Paper of that Powder?

An. In our Garret; the same night I brought it over.

Qu. Was any Body there when you gave it to her?

An. No.

Qu. What did she do with it?

An. She took it & put it upon the Table.

Qu. Did you give her the whole of the Powder you had of Robbin the first Time?

An. Yes. I gave her the Paper with all the Powder in it, as I received it of Robbin.

Qu. Did you tell her what was in the Paper?

An. No. She knew what was in it; for she told me what to get.

Qu. What did she tell you to get?

An. Something to kill three Pigs.

Qu. Did Robbin give you any Directions how to use that Powder, and tell you what Effect it would have?

Ans. He told me to put it into about 2 Quarts of Swill or Indian meal, and it would make 'em swell up.

Qu. Did you tell her how she must use the Powder? or what Effect it would have?

Answr. yes I told her as Robbin told me.

Qu. Do you know whether she used that Powder or any Part of it?

Answr. no otherwise than as Phœbe & Phillis told me Since my master's Death.

Qu. Who did you give the Second Paper of Powder to?

An. To Phillis.

Qu. When & where did you give that Paper of Powder to Phillis?

Ans. In the little House; She came to empty a Pot over the Wharffe, and I gave it to her, The Monday before my sd. Master died, after Breakfast in the Forenoon.

Qu: Did you then give her all the Powder you recd. of Robbin the Second Time?

Ans. Yes. I took off the brown Paper and gave it to her in the white Paper, that it was in, when Robbin gave it to me.

Qu. What did she do with it?

Answr. She caried it into the House to Phœbe as Phillis told me, She came to me & told me Phœbe sent her for that Thing that She sent me for, and thereupon I gave Phillis the Paper.

Qu: How was your Master poisoned with these Powders?

Answr. Phœbe & Phillis told me that they used them for that End.

Qu: When did they tell you this?

Answr. The next Day after my master died.

Q: Were they together when they told you So?

Answr. No, Phillis told me of it first, and said that Phœbe used all that I brought first, that Way; and that the last was used so too by her and Phœbe; and then I went to Phœbe and ask'd her about it, and She denyed it at first but when I told her that Phillis had told me all about it, then she owned it.

Quest. Had you no Reason before your sd. master dyed to think that the Powders you had of Robbin were given to your master or that he was poison'd therewith?

Answr. No other Reason than hearing Phœbe the Saturday night before master died ask Phillis, if she had given him enough, to which she replyed, yes. I have given him enough, and will stick as close to him as his shirt to his back; but who she meant I did not then know, nor untill after master died.

Quest. Was there no Discourse had between you Phœbe & Phillis about getting more Poison, after you had the first, of Robbin?

Answ. The Fryday before my master died Phœbe told me that she had lost that stuff that I had brought to her from Robbin, and desired me to get her some more. I told her I wou'd when I went over to Boston; this was in the Forenoon, when she was washing in the back yard.

Quest. Did you get her any more of Robbin?

Ansr. Yes, and that was it which I gave to Phillis

Quest. When did you go over to get the last Poison?

Ans. on the Saturday night before my master died; I went over after Sunset; I went directly to Robbin; & told him I wanted some of the same I had of him before for that was lost, Robbin was then at the Corner of his master's House out in the street, he told me he could not get any then, but if I wou'd come on the Sabbath Day night he would let me have some, and I went to him on the Sabbath Day night after Candle Light, and he then gave it to me.

Quest. Was there any Body with you on the Saturday night when you ask'd for the Poison, or do you know whether any Person saw you & Robbin together that Evening?

Answr. No, nobody was there, and I dont know that any Body saw us together that Evening.

Quest. How long was you with Robbin at Mr. Harris's Work house?

Answr. I made no tarry there, but left him at the Pot house, and he and the young man that was with him followed me and overtook me a little below Mr. Waite's Slaughter house; And they went with me into the Lane leading from the market Place to the long Wharffe near Mrs. Shearman's, while I went into Mrs. Shearmans and got a mug of Toddy, in the mug I brought from Mr. Harris's Work house, and I carried it to them and they both drank with me.

Quest. Had you any Discourse with Robbin in private or between you and him alone that Day?

Ansr. No, none at all.

Quest. Where did you drink the Toddy?

Answr. In the Lane aforesd.

Quest. Where did you all go after you drank the Toddy?

Answr. We all came away together & went thro' Mr. Sprague's Yard & so thro' Mrs. Silence Harris's yard & Entry into the street. and they went directly down to the Ferry and I went into my master's Yard with the Pots I brought from the Potters Work house.

Quest. Did you then go with them to the Ferry or nearer to it than your master's House?

Answr. No, I did not.

Quest. Did Robbin give you, or did you give Robbin any Thing between the Time of your coming out of Mr. Harris's Entry and his going over the Ferry?

Answr. No, I did not give him any Thing neither did he give me any Thing.

Quest. After you had parted with him when you came thro' the Entry, did you call him back?

Answr. No, I did not.

Quest. Did your master that Day forbid Mrs Shearman's letting you have any more Drink?

Answr. Yes, my master told her not to sell any Drink to any of his Servants.

Quest. Did Robbin know of it?

Answr. Not that I know of; he see master go into Mrs. Shearman's Shop, and pass'd by Robbin in the Lane as Robbin told me.

Quest. Did you ever apply to any body else, besides Robbin for Poison?

Answr. No, only to Carr, Doctr. Gibbon's negro man, and then Phœbe sent me for it. She had been with Carr before on the same account, & he told her he cou'd not get her any then, as she told me;

Quest. Did you get any Poison of Carr?

Ansr. No, he told me he wou'd not let me have any, untill he had seen Quaco, and did not know whether he shou'd then or not, and I never went to him afterwards.

Quest. Did you never ask Doctr. Rand's Cato for any Poison?

Answr. No, I do not know that I ever did, in the World.

Quest. Had you and Phœbe any Conversation together about your master in or near your Blacksmith's Shop or in the yard the Monday before your master died?

Answr. I had not, that I know of.

Quest. Did you that Day before Tom or any other of your master's Servants say that you knew that your master would dye or utter any Words to that effect?

Answr. No, I did not. The Day before master dyed, Phœbe came into the Shop to dress Tom's Eye & got to dancing & mocking master & shaking herself & acting as master did in the Bed; And Tom said he did not care, he hop'd he wou'd never get up again for his Eye's sake, and Scipio was there at the same time and saw her.

Quest. Did you ever Say that your master had been offer'd £400 for you but wou'd not take it, and now he shou'd not have a farthing or Words to that effect?

Answr. No I never said any such Thing. MARK.[1]

Quest. Did you ever tell Phœbe or Phillis that the Week before your master dyed, that you went over the Ferry to see Robbin to get some more Poison, and that he came over the Ferry in another Boat and so you mist each other and that he Robbin pretended to the Ferry-man that he was a Country negro and wanted to see you about your Child, or Words to that Effect?

Answr. I never told them or either of them so.

Quest. How came that Viall buried near your Forge in the Black-Smith's Shop, that you told Mr. Kettell of, and he found there?

Answr. I buried it there.

Quest. When did you bury it there?

Answr. In the afternoon of that Day that master dyed.

Quest. Where did you get that Vial?

Answr. I took it from Phillis that same Afternoon.

Quest. Did any body see you take it from her?

Answr. No. When I took it from Phillis she own'd that Phœbe had given the first Poison that I brought to master; and that she and Phœbe had given him all the Rest saving what was then in the Bottle. and thereupon I went to Phœbe and charged her with it, she at first deny'd it, but at last own'd it it and begg'd me to say nothing about it; I told her if I had known she wou'd have put it to that use I would not have got it for her; then I call'd Pompey to go down to the shop with me for I wanted to speak with him, intending to shew him the Vial, and he came into the shop but before I had an opportunity to speak to him Mr. Kettell took me.

Quest. Where was the Vial when you talked with Phœbe as aforesd?

Answr. I had it in my Pocket, and told her so, then I went into the shop and buried it, then I went into the House immediately to call Pompey to shew it to him.

Quest. Why did you bury the Vial before you called Pompy? or shew it to any body?

Answr: I buried it because I did not want any body should see it before I shewed it to him.

Questn. Have you lately had any Potters powder'd Lead by you or in your Possession?

Answr. Only that I had from Essex Powars; which was as I suppose ground to Powder.

Quest. When did you get that powder'd Lead of Essex?

Ansr: I had it of him that Day I went there for six butter Pots, which my master's son Isaac sent me for.

Quest. What did you get that Lead for?

Answr. To see if it would melt in our Fire. upon a Dispute between Tom and I about it; Tom said it would melt, and I told him I did not believe it would; I carried it home and laid it upon the Wall Plate in the Blacksmith's shop, and I never moved it afterwards or thought any Thing about it, 'till it was show'd to me by the Justice.

Quet. Do you know that any Part of that Lead you had of Essex or any Lead like unto it was given to your master or put into his Victuals or Drink?

Answr. I do not.

Quest. Do you know of any Proposal made of poisoning your master?

Answ. No, I do not, nor ever heard any such Thing proposed by any Body.

Quest. Do you know of any Cushoe nuts being procured for that Purpose?

Answr. No; I have not seen a Cushoe nut since I have been in this Country.

Quest. Do you know of any Copperas or Green stuff being provided for that Purpose?

Answr. No I do not.

Quest. What Time on the Saturday before your master dyed was it that you heard Phœbe ask Phillis, if she had given him enough, and Phillis said she had, and would stick as close to him as his Shirt to his Back?

Answr. In the afternoon about Dark; and before I went to Boston.

Quest. How came you, after you had heard this Talk between Phœbe and Phillis, to get her sd. Phœbe more Poison?

Answr. I did not know what she meant by their Talk, nor who they meant, by him.

Quest. Did you tell Carr that Phœbe sent you for that Poison you applyed to him for?

Answr. She did not tell me it was Poison, but told me to ask Carr for that Thing he had promised her; he said he knew what it was and would not send it, 'till he had talked to Quaco, and did not know that he should send it afterwards; and I said no more to Carr about it.

Quest. Did you ever ask Carr at any other Time for Poison?

Ansr. No.

Quest. Did you never ask him for something to Poison or kill a Dog?

Answr. No, not that I know of.

Quest. Was you ever bit by a Dog?

Answr. No. I never was.

Quest. Do you know any Thing more of your master's being poisoned than you have before related?

Ansr. No, I do not.

MARK.

[Bill of Indictment.]

MIDDLESEX ss.	His Majesties Superiour Court of Judicature Court of Assize and General Goal Delivery held at Cambridge in and for the County of Middlesex on the first Tuesday of August in the Twenty ninth Year of the Reign of George the Second by the Grace of God of Great Britain France & Ireland King Defender of the Faith &c.

The Jurors for the said Lord the King upon their Oath present That Phillis a Negro woman of Charlestown in the County of Middlesex Spinster Servant of John Codman late of Charlestown aforesaid Gentleman not having the Fear of God before her Eyes but of her Malice forethought contriving to deprive the said John Codman her said Master of his Life and him feloniously and Traiterously to kill and murder, She the said Phillis on the thirtieth Day of June last at Charlestown aforesaid in the Dwelling house of the said John there did of her Malice forethought willfully feloniously and Traiterously put a Deadly Poison called Arsenick into a Vial of water and thereby did then and there Poison the same Water——and that the said Phillis knowing the Water aforesaid to be so poisoned did then and there feloniously willfully traiterously and of her Malice forethought put one spoonfull of the Same Water so poisoned into a Pint of the Said John's Watergruel and thereby poison the Same Watergruel——And that the said Phillis did then and there of her malice forethought feloniously willfully and traiterously in manner as aforesaid poison the Watergruel aforesaid, with a felonious and Traiterous Intent and Design that the said John her said master then being should then and there eat the Same Watergruel so poisoned and thereby be poisoned killed & murdered——And that one Elizabeth Codman not knowing the Watergruel aforesaid to be so poisoned then and there Innocently gave the Same Watergruel so poisoned as aforesaid to the said John to eat—

And that the said John then and there being the said Phillis's Master and being altogether ignorant of the Watergruel aforesaid's being poisoned as as[2] aforesaid and Suspecting no Evil did then and there eat the same Watergruel so poisoned as aforesaid——And that the said Phillis then and there was feloniously and traiterously present with the said Elizabeth & John knowing of and consenting unto the said Elizabeth's giving him the said John the Watergruel aforesaid so poisoned as aforesaid and his eating the same as aforesaid——And that the said John by means of his eating the Watergruel aforesaid so poisoned as aforesaid There Languished for the space of fifteen Hours and then at Charlestown aforesaid Died of the Poison aforesaid given him as aforesaid——And So the Jurors aforesaid upon their Oath say that the said Phillis did at Charlestown aforesaid of her malice forethought in manner and form aforesaid willfully feloniously and traiterously poison kill & murder the said John Codman her said master against the Peace of the said Lord the King his Crown & Dignity.

And the Jurors aforesaid upon their Oath further present That Mark a Negro man of Charlestown aforesaid Labourer and Servant of the said John Codman. And Robbin a Negro man of Boston in the County of Suffolk Labourer & Servant of John Clark of Boston aforesaid Apothecary before the said Treason and murder aforesaid committed by the said Phillis in manner & form aforesaid did at Charlestown aforesaid on the twentieth Day of June last of their malice forethought (the said Mark then being Servant of the said John Codman) feloniously & traiterously advise & incite procure & abet the said Phillis to do and commit the said Treason & Murder aforesaid against the Peace of the said Lord the King his Crown and Dignity.

EDM TROWBRIDGE *Attr* ℞ *Dom Rege.*

This is a True Bill.
CALEB DANA *foreman.*

The case was tried, at the same term at which the parties were indicted, before Stephen Sewall, chief justice, and Benjamin Lynde, John Cushing, and Chambers Russell, associate justices,—all fairly read in the law, and the Chief Justice eminent in his profession. Samuel Winthrop and Nathaniel Hatch, jointly, were clerks of the court.[3]

Mark and Phillis were convicted, and sentence of death was pronounced upon them in strict conformity to the common law of England. On the 6th of September, a warrant for their execution was issued, under the seal of the court, commanding Richard Foster, Sheriff of Middlesex, to perform the last office of the law, on the 18th of the same month; and upon this warrant the sheriff made return upon the day of the execution.

The subpœnas to the witnesses against the accused, the caption and conclusion of the record of the case, and the warrant for the execution of the condemned are as follows:—

PROVINCE OF THE MASSACHUSETTS BAY, ss. } } }	ge *the Second by the Grace of God of Great Britain France & Ireland King Defender of ye Faith &c.*
SEAL.	the Sheriff of our County of Middlesex his under Sheriff or Deputy or to any Constable of the Town of Charlestown within Said County, Greeting—

We Command you That you Su[=m]on Wm. Brattle Esqr Docter Pinchin of Boston Joseph Rand Junr. Hatter Bartholomew Powers Isaac Rand Phisitian Wm. Kneland, Benjn. Codman Parnel Codman Elizh. Codman Mary Codman Ann Codman Catherine Codman, Pompey Thomas Cuffee and Scipeo negro servants that were Jno. Codman Decd. James Kittle Wm. Foster Phisitian Essex Servant to thomas powers Servt. of Dr. Rand Dinah Servt. of Richd. Foster Esqr Ruth Adams

To appear Before our Justices of our Superiour Court of Judicature Court of Assize and General Goal Delivery now held at Cambridge within & for said County tomorrow at Eight of ye Clock before noon to give Such Evidence in our Behalf (as you know) against Mark a Negro man & Phillis a Negro woman both of Charlestown aforesaid—

Hereof fail not and so soon as may be make return of this Writ with your Doings Therein into the same Court Witness Stephen Sewall Esq. at Boston the sixth Day of August in the twenty ninth year of our Reign Annoq. Domini 1755

SAML WINTHROP *Cler*

[*Endorsed Return.*]

MIDDLESEX ss. August 7, 1755

We have somoned the persons within named to appear & Give Evidence at the time & place within mentioned.

JAMES KETTELL, *Dept Sheriff,*
& JOHN MILLER
Constabel.

PROVINCE OF THE MASSACHUSETTS BAY, ss	} }	ge the Second by the Grace of God of Great Britain France & Ireland King Defender of the Faith &c.

SEAL.	he Sheriff of our County of Suffolk his under Sheriff or Deputy or any Constable of the Town of Boston in sd. County Greeting

We Command you that you Summon The Wife of Ichabod Jones Eliza. Mercy Car, a negro man servant of John Gibbins Apothecary Quaco the servt. of —— Dalton Quaco a Negro man belonging to mr. John White

To appear before our Justices of our Superiour Court of Judicature Court of Assize & General Goal Delivery now holden at Cambridge within and for said County Tomorrow morning at Eight of ye Clock before noon Then and there to give Such Evidence in our Behalf as you know against Mark a Negro man & Phillis a Negro woman both of Charlestown in our County of Middlesex—

Hereof Fail not and so soon as may be make Return of this Writ with your Doings therein into the same Court

Witness Stephen Sewall Esq. at Boston the Sixth Day of August in the twenty ninth year of our Reign Annoq, Domini 1755

SAML WINTHROP *Cler*

[Record of the Case.]

| PROVINCE OF THE MASSACHUSETTS BAY MIDDLESEX ss. | } } } | *Regni Regis Georgii secondi Magnæ Britanniæ Franciæ Hiberniæ vicesimonono.* |

At his Majestys Superiour Court of Judicature Court of Assize and General Goal Delivery began and held at Cambridge within and for the County of Middlesex on the first Tuesday of August Annoque Domini 1755—

By the Honoble. Stephen Sewall Esqr: Chief Justice
Benjamin Lynde[4] }
John Cushing &} Esquires Justices
Chambers Russell }

[*After reciting the words of the indictment, the record proceeds as follows, being, as far as where the record of the trial and sentence begins, an extension of a memorandum on the indictment.*]

Upon this Indictment the said Phillis was arraigned and upon her arraignment pleaded not guilty and for trial put herself upon God and the Country and the said Mark was also arraigned upon this Indictment and upon his arraignment pleaded not Guilty and for trial put himself upon God and the Country, a Jury was thereupon Sworne to try the issue Mr. John Miller Foreman and fellows who having fully heared the Evidence went out to consider thereof and returned with their verdicts and upon their oath's say'd that the said Phillis is Guilty, and that the said Mark is Guilty, upon which the prisoners were remanded, and being again brot and set to the Bar, the Kings Attorney moved the Court that Judgment of Death might be given against them, whereupon they were asked by the chief Justice if they had ought to say why Judgment of Death should not be given against them, and having nothing material to offer Judgment of Death was pronounced against them by the chief Justice in the name of the Court in form following that is to Say that the said Phillis go from hence to the place where she came from, and from thence to the place of Execution & there be burnt to Death, and that the said Mark go from hence to the place where he came from, and from thence be drawn to the place of Execution and there be hanged by the neck until he be dead and God Almighty have mercy upon their Souls. Ordered that these Sentences be put into Execution upon thursday the eighth[5] day of September next between the hours of one and five of the Clock in the Afternoon.

Warrant issued Sep. 6. 1755.

[Writ of execution, or death-warrant.]

| PROVINCE OF THE MASSACHUSETTS BAY MIDDLESEX ss. | } } } | ge the second by the Grace of God of Great Britain France & Ireland King Defender of the Faith &Ca |

SEAL.   Richard Foster Esqr. Sheriff of our County of Middlesex in Said Province

Greeting

Whereas at our Superiour Court of Judicature Court of Assize and General Goal Delivery begun and held at Cambridge within and for the County of Middlesex on the first Tuesday of August last the Grand Jurors for us for the Body of our said County of Middlesex did on their Oath Present That Phillis a Negro woman of Charlestown in the County of Middlesex Spinster Servant of John Codman late of Charlestown aforesaid Gentleman, not having the fear of God before her Eyes, but of her malice forethought contriving to deprive the Said John Codman her Said master of his life and him feloniously and Traiterously to kill and murder, she the said Phillis on the thirteenth day of June last at Charlestown aforesaid in the dwelling house of the said John there did of her malice forethought willfully felloniously and Traiterously put a Deadly Poison called Arsenick into a Vial of Water and thereby did then and there Poison the same water—and That the said Phillis knowing the water aforesaid to be so poisoned did then and there feloniously willfully traiterously and of her malice forethought put one spoonfull of the same water so poisoned into a pint of the said John's watergruel and thereby poison the same watergruel—and that the said Phillis did then and there of her malice forethought felloniously willfully & traiterously in manner as aforesaid poison the watergruel aforesaid, with a felonious and traiterous Intent and design that the said John her said master then being should then and there eat the Same Watergruel so poisoned and thereby be Poisoned killed and murdered. And that one Elizabeth Codman not knowing the watergruel aforesaid to be so poisoned then and there Innocently gave the Same Watergruel so poisoned as aforesaid to the Said John to eat, and that the Said John then and there being the said Phillis's master and being altogether Ignorant of the watergruel aforesaid's being poisoned as aforesaid and suspecting no Evil did then & there eat the same watergruel so poisoned as aforesaid & that the said Phillis then and there was feloniously and traiterously present with the said Elizabeth & John knowing of & consenting unto the sd. Elizabeth's giving him the said John the watergruel aforesd. so poisoned as aforesaid & his eating the same as aforesd. And that the said John by means of his eating the watergruel aforesaid so poisoned as aforesaid there Languished for the space of Fifteen hours & then at Charlestown aforesaid died of the Poison aforesd. given him as aforesaid—and so the Jurors aforesaid upon their Oath said that the said Phillis did at Charlestown aforesaid of her malice forethought in manner and form aforesaid willfully feloniously and traiterously poison kill & murder the said John Codman her Said master against our Peace Crown & Dignity, and The Jurors aforesaid upon their Oath further present That Mark a Negroman of Charlestown aforesaid Labourer and Servant of the said John Codman before the said Treason and murder aforesaid committed by the said Phillis in manner and form aforesaid did at Charlestown aforesaid on the twentieth day of June last of his malice forethought (the said Mark then being Servant of the said John Codman) felloniously & traiterously advise and incite procure & abet the Said Phillis to do & commit the said Treason & murder aforesaid against our peace crown & Dignity (as in Said Indictmt. is at large Set forth) upon which Indictment the said Phillis and Mark were Severally arraigned and upon their arraignment Severally pleaded not Guilty and for Tryal put themselves on God and the Country, and Whereas the said Phillis & Mark at our Court aforesaid were each of them convict of the crime respectively alledg'd to be committed by them as aforesaid by the Verdict of twelve good & lawful men of our Said County and were by the consideration of our Said Court adjudged to Suffer the Pains of Death therefor; as to us appears of Record Execution of which said Sentence doth still remain to be done we command you therefore that on Thursday the Eighteenth day of September instant between the hours of one & Five o'Clock in the day time you cause the said Phillis to be drawn from our Goal in our County of Middlesex aforesaid (where she now is) to the place of Execution and there be burnt to Death & also that on the Same day between the hours of one & five of the Clock in the day time you cause the Said Mark to be drawn from our Goal in our County of Middlesex aforesaid (where he now is) to the place of Execution & there be hanged up by the Neck until he be dead, & for so doing this shall be your Sufficient Warrant—Hereof fail not; and make Return of this writ with your doings therein into the Clerks Office of our Said Court as soon as may be after you have Executed the Same Witness Stephen Sewall Esqr: at Boston the sixth day of September in the Twenty ninth Year of our reign Annoque Domini 1755—

By Order of Court

NATHANIEL HATCH *Cler*

MIDDLESEX. ss—September the 18th. 1755.

I Executed this warrant as above directed, by causing Phillis to be burnt to Death, and Mark to be hang'd by the neck until he was dead, between the hours of one and five a Clock of Said day—

RICHD. FOSTER *Sheriff*

It is worthy of observation that no such process as a formal warrant was required for a capital execution by the laws of England. In the King's Bench, the prisoner was committed to the custody of the marshal at the beginning of the trial, and an award of judgment upon the record was all the authority that that officer had for the execution. Formerly, it was customary in courts of oyer and terminer, and of jail delivery, to authorize the execution by a precept under the hands and seals of three or more commissioners, of whom one, at least, should be of the quorum; but this custom had become obsolete at the time of this trial, and only a calendar, or abstract of the record, subscribed by the judge, was put into the hands of the sheriff for this purpose; and such is the practice in England, I presume, to this day.

Even Blackstone, who is so blind to many gross imperfections in the jurisprudence of his native country, is forced to remark, in view of the looseness of procedure in capital cases,—

"It may certainly afford matter of speculation that in civil causes there should be such a variety of writs of execution to recover a trifling debt, issued in the king's name, and under the seal of the court, without which the sheriff cannot legally stir one step; and yet that the execution of a man, the most important and terrible task of any, should depend upon a marginal note."[6]

The courts and people of New England were always more mindful of the sacredness of human life than those of other nations, save, perhaps, the little community of the Netherlands. They also attached great importance to the formal proceedings by which the ends of justice were reached in criminal cases. This is well illustrated by an incident that is recorded relative to the action of the judges of the Superior Court of the Province when, after the conviction of Richardson for the murder of the boy Sneider, in 1770, it became evident to them that the cause of justice required that they should intercede to prevent his execution. They were long in doubt as to the sufficiency of a pardon obtained from the crown through the recommendation of the Lieutenant-Governor upon their certificate of its propriety, the only evidence of the pardon being its insertion in the Newgate Calendar. Hutchinson relates that "they were at length satisfied; and the prisoner having been brought into court early in the morning, when scarcely anybody but the officers of the court were present, pleaded his Majesty's pardon, and was discharged, and immediately absconded."[7]

But, to proceed with a definition of the crime committed by these negroes, and a more particular account of the punishment for petit treason:—

By the statute 25 Edw. III., this crime, which had had a wider application, was restricted to three classes of cases: 1, where a servant killed his master or mistress; 2, where a wife killed her husband; 3, where a clergyman killed his prelate, or the superior to whom he owed canonical obedience. The sentence in the case of a woman was, that she be burned to death, and in the case of a man, that he be drawn to the place of execution and there hanged by the neck until he be dead.[8] To mitigate the sufferings of felons at the stake, the executioner usually fastened one end of a cord to the stake, and bringing this cord around the neck of the woman, pulled it tightly the moment the torch was applied, and continued the strain until life was extinct, which, unless the cord was sooner burnt asunder, generally happened before the condemned had suffered much from the intensity of the flames.

In cases of high treason, other barbarities were practised upon the bodies of the criminals, but these were frequently, and in cases of persons of distinction, generally, remitted. Indeed, even the hanging was dispensed with in these latter cases; and hence we read of the execution of great prisoners of state, male and female, by beheading, which, strictly, is a manner of death unknown to the laws of England, except as an incident to the principal penalty by hanging or burning. After the hanging, the body, according to rule, was to be cut down (if possible, while yet alive) to be eviscerated, then beheaded, and the trunk and limbs divided into four parts, to be disposed of as the sovereign should order. By special writ, under the privy seal, all these circumstances, except decapitation, were, as I have already said, usually omitted.

All male persons convicted whether of high treason or of petit treason were, unless specially exempted in the manner I have stated, *drawn* to the place of execution. This was originally an ignominious incident of the terrible penalty, and required that the criminal should be rudely pulled along over the ground, behind a horse; later, however, a hurdle or wicker frame, or a sledge,—that is, as we call it, a sled,—was used, either from motives of humanity, or in order to prolong the life of the traitor through subsequent stages of the punishment. According to Sir Matthew Hale, women were not to be drawn, in cases of petit treason, although the practice of later times, certainly, was to the contrary.[9] However, after the repeal in 1790, of the law for burning women, for which drawing and hanging were then substituted, women as well as men were sentenced to be drawn to the place of execution.

Another incident to this punishment, though not peculiar to it, since it applied to all atrocious felonies, was the gibbeting, or hanging in chains. This was no part of the sentence, but was performed in accordance with a special order or direction of the court, given, probably, in most cases, verbally to the sheriff. After execution, the body of the felon was taken from the gallows and hung upon a gibbet conveniently near the place where the fact was committed, there to remain, until, from the action of the elements, or the ravages of birds of prey, it disappeared. Of the object of this ghastly feature of capital punishment it is alleged, "besides the terror of the example," "that it is a comfortable sight to the friends and relations of the deceased"; but the obviousness of this reason is somewhat lessened by the doubt in which we are left as to which deceased person, the criminal or his victim, is referred to. In the case of Mark it is noticeable that no sentence to the gibbet appears in the record, and I have found no order for it, or mention of it, in the papers on file.

Phillis and Mark were executed at the usual place of execution in Cambridge; and the following account of the affair is taken from the Boston "Evening Post," of Sept. 22, 1755:—

"Thursday last, in the Afternoon, *Mark*, a Negro Man, and *Phillis*, a Negro Woman, both Servants to the late Capt. *John Codman*, of *Charlestown*, were executed at *Cambridge*, for poisoning their said Master, as mentioned in this Paper some Weeks ago. The Fellow was hanged, and the Woman burned at a Stake about Ten Yards distant from the Gallows. They both confessed themselves guilty of the Crime for which they suffered, acknowledged the Justice of their Sentence, and died very penitent. After Execution, the Body of *Mark* was brought down to *Charlestown* Common, and hanged in Chains, on a Gibbet erected there for that Purpose."

Frothingham, in his "History of Charlestown,"[10] quotes this item from the "Post," and adds, from Dr. Josiah Bartlett's account of Charlestown,[11] that "the place where Mark was suspended in irons was on the northerly side of Cambridge Road, about one fourth of a mile above our peninsula." He also adds, from the same authority, that "Phebe, who was the most culpable," became evidence against the others, and that she was transported to the West Indies.

It is very likely that Phebe was transported, as described by Dr. Bartlett, but there is nothing on record to show that she was used as a principal witness. Indeed, the answers of Phillis and Mark on their examination are mutually recriminative, and amount to a plenary confession of the crime of each. Besides, as neither the governor nor the court had any authority to grant a pardon for murder,[12] it is not likely that any favor was shown to her in accordance with a promise from either, nor is there any evidence that any lenity was actually extended to her, except the negative circumstance that she was not included in the indictment.

This completes the narrative of this remarkable case. The body of Mark is said by Dr. Bartlett to have remained on the gibbet "until a short time before the Revolution." Certain it is that when Dr. Caleb Rea passed through Charlestown on the first day of June, 1758, on his way from Danvers to join the regiment, of which he had been chosen surgeon, in the expedition against Ticonderoga, he found the body hanging, and, having examined it, recorded in his journal that "his [Mark's] skin was but very little broken, although he had hung there near three or four years."[13]

Finally, another patriot,—Paul Revere,—in describing his famous ride on the 18th of April, 1775, on a still more important errand, says, "After I had passed Charlestown Neck, and got nearly opposite where *Mark was hung in chains*, I saw two men on horseback under a tree,"[14] &c.; thus alluding to the site of the gibbet as a place well known at that time,—as undoubtedly it was, to all the country round.

I have said that this is the only case of petit treason to be found in our records. There was, indeed, an earlier case in which the penalty of death by burning was inflicted; but in regard to that case there is no suggestion anywhere to my knowledge that the crime of petit treason had been committed, nor any allegation to that effect in the charge or indictment, nor even a hint that any life was lost by the misconduct of the condemned.[15] This was the case of Maria, a negress, who was executed at Roxbury in 1681. Perhaps it will be well to give the story of this case as it appears on the records of the Court of Assistants.[16]

"Marja[17] Negro Servant to Joshua Lambe of Roxbury in the County of Suffolk in New England being presented by the Grand Jury was Indicted by the name of Marja Negro for not hauing the feare of God before hir eyes & being Instigated by the divil at or upon the eleventh Day of July last in the night did wittingly willingly & felloniously set on fier the dwelling house of Thomas Swann of sd Roxbury by taking a coale from vnder a still & carrjed it into another Roome and layd it on floore neere the doore & presently went & crept into a hole at a back doore of thy master Lambs house & set it on fier also taking a liue coale betweene two chips & carried it into the chimber by which also it was Consumed as by yr Confession will appeare Contrary to the peace of our Soueraigne Lord the king his croune & dignity the lawes of this Jurisdiction in that Case made & prouided title firing of houses—The prisoner at the barr pleaded & acknowledged hirselfe to be Guilty of ye fact. And accordingly the next day being Again brought to the Barr had sentenc of death pronnonc't agt hir by the Honnoble Gouñor. that she should Goe from the barr to the prison whenc she came & thence to the place of execution & there be burnt.—Ye lord be mercifull to thy Soule sd ye Gov."

The case was capital under the act referred to in the record. The act reads as follows:—

Burning Houses.

And if any person of the age aforesaid, [16 years and upwards] shall after the publication hereof, wittingly and willingly, and felloniously, set on fire any *Dwelling House, Meeting House, Store House*, or shall in like manner, set on fire any *out-House, Barn, Stable, Leanto, Stack of Hay, Corn or Wood*, or any thing of like nature, whereby any *Dwelling House, Meeting House or Store House* cometh to be burnt, the party or parties vehemently suspected thereof, shall be apprehended by **Capital.**Warrant from one or more of the Magistrates, and committed to Prison, there to remain without Baile, till the next Court of Assistants, who upon legal conviction by due proof, or confession of the Crime, shall adjudge such person or persons to be put to death, and to forfeit so much of his Lands, Goods or Chattels, as shall make full satisfaction, to the party or parties damnified. [1652.][18]

It will be observed that the law prescribes no such punishment as was ordered by the Assistants, and how the court were satisfied of the legality of their sentence is to me inexplicable, except upon the possible claim that they might rightfully exercise the expansive discretion which they applied to the case of the first Quakers, and so supply a deficiency in the ordinances of the General Court, by administering the *lex talionis*[19] in this particular instance as a necessary terror to evil-doers.

The public opinion which permitted the colonial magistrates to exercise, unchallenged, a discretion not given to them by positive law, as in this case and that of the first Quakers, and in the instance of their conviction of a capital crime, of Tom, the Indian, in 1674,[20] of whose guilt the jury were doubtful, cannot be deemed to have enlarged their authority, by *custom*, without a perversion of language and a disregard of fundamental distinctions relative to the nature and source of law.[21]

Two other negroes who were suspected of complicity with Maria were ordered to be transported. The record is as follows:—

"Chessaleer negros Sentence"

Chessaleer negro servant to Tho. Walker brickmaker now in Goale on suspition of Joyning wth Marja Negro in Burning of Dr Swans' & —— Lambs houses in Roxbury in July last The Court on Consideration of the Case Judged it meet to order that he be kept in prison till his master send him out of the country & then dischardg ye charges of Imprisonment wch if he refuse to doe aboue one moneth the country Tresurer is to see it donne & when ye chardges be defrayd to returne the ouerplus to ye sd Walker

**James Pembertons
negro sentence**

The like Judgment & sentenc was declard against James Pemberton's negro in all respects as agt Chessaleer negro &c.[22]

Still another negro was convicted, at the same term of the court, of the crime of arson, and ordered to be hanged, and afterwards consumed to ashes in the same fire with Maria, as appears by the following record:—

"Jack negro servant to Mr Samuel Woolcot of Weathersfield thou art Jndicted by the name of Jack Negro for not hauing the feare of God before thy eyes being Instigated by the Divill did at or upon the foureteenth day of July last 1681 wittingly & felloniously sett on fier Leifteñat Wm Clarks house in North Hampton. by taking

**Jack negro
Jndicted & sentenc**

a brand of fier from the hearth and swinging it vp & doune for to find victualls as by his confession may Appeare Contrary to the peace of our Soueraigne Lord the King his Croune & dignity the lawes of God & of this Jurisdiction in that case made & prouided title firing of houses page (52) to wch Jndictment at the barr he pleaded not Guilty, & Affirmd he would be trjed by God & the Country and after his Confessions &c. were read to him & his owni[=g] thereof were Comitted to the Jury who brought him in Guilty and the next day had his sentence pronounct agt him by the Gouernor that he should goe from the barr to the place whence he came & there be hangd by the neck till he be dead & then taken doune & burnt to Ashes in the fier wth Marja Negro—The Lord be mercifull to thy soule sajd the Gouernor"[23]

There was some excuse for the latter part of this sentence, for since the offence was an atrocious felony, such as in England would subject the offender to an infamous punishment, it seemed proper to attach something more of ignominy to his sentence than the mere execution by hanging.

Our forefathers of the colonial period regarded the Mosaic law as of too sacred obligation to be impaired in the least degree; much more to be expressly contravened by the courts of justice in respect to the command,—

"And if a man have committed a sin worthy of death, and he be to be put to death, and thou hang him on a tree, his body shall not remain all night upon the tree, but thou shalt in any wise bury him that day; (for he that is hanged is accursed of God;) that thy land be not defiled, which the Lord thy God giveth thee for an inheritance."[24]

—they, therefore, by an ordinance passed in 1641, had required that the body of every executed criminal should be buried within twelve hours after death, except in cases of anatomy, which prevented the possibility of hanging in chains after the English fashion; and the only way in which they could set a mark of infamy upon the deceased criminal, without a breach of the colonial ordinance as well as of the divine law, was to burn the body.[25]

But this tendency to a strict adherence to the laws of Israel disappeared early in the provincial period, under the operation of the same causes which led to the abandonment of those rugged metaphrases of the Psalms of David, and of the song of Deborah and Barak, &c., contained in the Bay Psalm-Book, for the smoother though less literal version of Tate and Brady and the presumptuous "Imitations" of Dr. Watts. When, therefore, under the new charter the offence called for it according to the custom of England, the gibbet was erected; and though the occasions for its employment were very rare, the report of sundry instances of its use has come down to us, as in the case of the pirates whose bodies hung in chains, from time to time, on the now vanished Bird Island in Boston Harbor, a locality as near the place where the fact was committed as could conveniently be used. I confess I find it impossible to understand whence the provincial judges claimed to derive their authority for ordering the bodies of criminals to be hung in chains. We have seen that, even if our fathers brought with them the right to exercise this authority, they soon enacted provisions entirely inconsistent with the practice; and I am not aware of any subsequent act of parliament, extending to the Colonies, that restored the authority; and certainly there was no law of the Province to that effect.

I ought not to dismiss this subject without adding something to the brief allusion already made to the comparative mildness of the laws of Massachusetts in respect to capital punishment. The execution of Mark and Phillis took place just about the time that Blackstone was delivering his lectures at Oxford, which have since given him an enduring and world-wide fame as a commentator on the laws of England. This elegant defender and apologist for English laws and customs, in his commentaries, admits, seemingly with reluctance and regret, that there then existed on the statute-books of England no less than one hundred and sixty capital offences. At that time the number of capital offences in Massachusetts was less than one-tenth this number, if we exclude those made so by the acts relating to military offenders in actual service, and felonies on the high seas, and a few others, which, like the latter, were created by including among capital crimes certain offences which, though theretofore exempt from the death penalty by special circumstances and technical rules, had always been capitally punished when committed under other and not less justifiable circumstances.

Said Isaac Backus, whom I find to be a very trustworthy authority, in a letter to this Society, under date of Feb. 20, 1794, "There has not been any person hanged in Plymouth County for above these sixty years past."[26] More than a century earlier, John Dunton mentions a sermon of Mather's, preached at the execution of "Morgan, the only person executed in that country [Massachusetts] for near seven years."[27] He must, however, I think, have forgotten the case of Maria, the negro woman.

Again, when the English riot act (1 Geo. I. stat. 2, ch. 5) was substantially adopted by the Province in 1751, the legislature studiously avoided the harshness of the former act by substituting forfeiture of lands and chattels, and whipping and imprisonment, for the death penalty.[28]

In 1761 Governor Bernard vainly labored with his utmost zeal to secure the passage of an act or acts making it felony, without benefit of clergy, to forge public and private securities or vouchers for money, or to coin or counterfeit the current money of the Province. He sent a special message upon the subject to the Assembly, in which he stated:—

"In regard to the popular prejudices against capital punishments which have hitherto prevailed in this country, I shall only say that at present they are very ill-timed. Whilst the people of this country lived from hand to mouth, and had very little wealth but what was confined among themselves, a simple system of laws might be proper, and capital punishments might in a great measure be avoided; but when by the acquisition, diffusion, and general intercourse of wealth, the temptations to fraud are abundantly increased, the terrors of it must be also proportionably enlarged; otherwise if, through a false tenderness for wicked men, the laws should not be sufficient to protect the property of the honest and industrious, the rights of the latter are given up to the former, and the undue mercy shown to the one becomes a real injury to the other. To instance this, I need only say that I have no doubt but that if these crimes had been capital some years ago, and usually punished as such, they would not have been committed at all at the present time."

The Governor's opinion, however, was not borne out by the experience of the British government in its dealings with crime. There, it was made a capital felony to steal in a dwelling-house to the amount of 40*s.*, or, privately, in a shop, goods to the value of 5*s.*, or to counterfeit stamps that were used for the sale of perfumery, or such as were used for the certificates of hair-powder; and yet, notwithstanding this severity, all who considered the subject thoughtfully found that the increase of capital crimes more than kept pace with the increase of laws creating them; and this became so alarmingly evident that at length the conservative opposition to reform was overborne, and Sir Samuel Romilly and his coadjutors began those changes which have continued in the same direction to the present day. Before the reform was established, however, executions became so frequent that it was not uncommon for citizens to avoid certain parts of London and its environs on account of the intolerable odor, there, of decaying human bodies, hung in chains by the highways and before the doors of citizens.

Still the judges rode their circuits, leaving briefly minuted "calendars" in the hands of the executioners, who erected close behind them the gallows and the gibbet as monuments of their dispensation of "justice." Barristers bandied repartees and cracked jokes over good dinners, and serjeants hobnobbed with their brethren of the bench and of the coif, apparently unconcerned at the responsible part they were enacting in this awful drama; while the poor rabble put on their best attire on the days of execution, and liberally patronized the venders of cakes and ale who, near the gallows, erected booths as on other gala days,—many of the spectators, no doubt, thinking that it would not be so bad a thing, after all, if it came their turn next to better their desperate condition by swinging on the newly contrived gallows, on which ten criminals could be hanged together.[29]

Alas! well may we ask with astonishment if it is possible that such a state of society really existed in the England of Hannah More, of Sir William Jones and Edmund Burke,—the land throughout which the Wesleys were preaching and singing to eager multitudes of the free grace and abounding mercy of God; where the pious Cowper was pleading for the relief of "insolvent innocence," and Clarkson and Wilberforce and Granville Sharp were rousing the public mind to the evils of slavery in distant colonies!

The case of petit treason which we have been considering occurred nine years before Beccaria startled all Europe with "the code of humanity,"—his treatise on crimes and punishments; yet had he known of our experience in this Province, he could have pointed to Massachusetts as the strongest practical illustration of the truth of his theory, that it is not necessary to multiply extreme penalties in order to prevent crime, but that we are to look for the amelioration of manners and the diminution of public and private wrongs to the mental and moral education of the people rather than to the terrors of the law.

In 1777, when the Revolutionary War was beginning to assume its gravest aspect, and when the hopes of traitors were reviving, the barbarous incidents of the punishment for treason were abolished by the legislature of Massachusetts, and this crime was made punishable simply by hanging. Eight years later the distinction between petit treason and murder was abolished,— an improvement of the criminal code in which we were followed by Great Britain five years later still.[30]

So that it was possible that our good city of Boston might have been disgraced by one of these horrible executions as late as 1785, and that a delicate woman could, with all the solemnity of legal forms, have been publicly burned to death at Tyburn as late as 1790!

In point of fact such executions occurred in England long after the burning of Phillis. A memorable case is that of Anne Beddingfield, who was burned for petit treason at Rushmore, near Ipswich, in 1763.

In 1813 the last of the minor infamous punishments, such as whipping, branding, the stocks, the pillory, cutting off ears, slitting noses, boring tongues, &c., were abolished in this Commonwealth.

As for hanging in chains, I cannot find when the custom was discontinued in Massachusetts. I do not remember to have read of an instance of this kind since the adoption of the Constitution, though I have made no special search for such an instance. Some of my hearers may be able to refer me definitely to the time and reason of the change.

In England, by the stat. 25 Geo. II., ch. 35 (1752), which was three years before the execution at Cambridge, provision was made that hanging in chains should be included in the sentence to be pronounced by the court against all persons convicted of murder, and that the sentence should be executed on the next day but one after it was pronounced. This was changed by the stat. 9 Geo. IV., ch. 31, so as to give the court a discretion to order hanging in chains or dissection; and the next year this act was extended to Ireland. By the stat. 2 & 3 Wm. IV., ch. 75, the court was authorized to order the body to be hung in chains or buried; and, finally, by the stat. 4 & 5 of Wm. IV., ch. 26 (July 25, 1834), all laws requiring bodies to be hung in chains were repealed.

No such sudden punishment as that prescribed by the act of parliament of the 25 Geo. II., could be legally inflicted here,—at least during the colonial period; for the colonial ordinance of 1641 required that four days at least should intervene between judgment and execution.

The only barbarous treatment of the bodies of criminals authorized by law in Massachusetts since the adoption of the Constitution, that I am aware of, was prescribed by the act of 1784, to discourage the practice of duelling, which revived some of the provisions of a law of the Province, passed in 1728, denying duellists the right to be buried in a coffin, and requiring the coroner or executioner to see that their bodies be interred near the place of execution, or in the public highway, with a stake driven through them.[31]

Now, happily, capital punishment is restricted in this Commonwealth and in England to two offences only; and while, here, even high treason is punishable simply by imprisonment, in England, strong efforts have been repeatedly made, and recently with a fair prospect of ultimate success, to induce parliament to imitate our example and take away the death penalty from this the highest crime known to the common law.

FOOTNOTES

[1] Mark signed his deposition here, and the entry, "continued," was made at the end of the sheet; the next sheet beginning, "Mark's Examination, continued."

[2] *Sic.*

[3] This is assumed to be the case, since both these clerks officially signed papers in this very case, though, from the loose custom which gradually obtained with the clerks of our highest judicial court, of not recording their appointments, it is impossible to verify this statement by the record. Samuel Tyley, Jr., and Benjamin Rolfe were sworn in as joint clerks of this court, Feb. 26, 1718, and Samuel Winthrop was clerk as early as June, 1745, and Nathaniel Hatch as early as September, 1752.

[4] Judge Lynde makes a memorandum of this trial, and of the particulars of the executions, in his diary under date of July 9, 1755.—Lynde Diaries (privately printed, 1880), p. 179.—EDS. OF PROCEEDINGS.

[5] An error. It should have been "eighteenth."

[6] Comm. book iv. ch. 32, p. 403.

[7] Hist. Mass. Bay, vol. iii. p. 287, n.

[8] By stat. 22 Hen. VIII. ch. 9, a person of either sex, who was convicted of murdering another by poison, was to be boiled to death, and the offence was, by the same act, declared high treason; but this act was repealed by 1 Edw. VI. ch. 12, after several executions under it, including that of Margaret Davy, who poisoned her mistress. Though by the common law poisoning was deemed a most atrocious circumstance, it did not alter the punishment of the principal crime involved. The law considered only the crime, and not the manner in which it was committed.

[9] The law was uncertain; but Hale appears to be the safest authority. Wood, in his Institutes,—at the time of this trial the most recent and popular treatise upon the laws of England,—states that women were to be drawn, in petit treason; as, indeed, do most, if not all, succeeding writers. They follow Coke, 3 Inst. 211; but neither the statutes referred to, nor the case cited from 12 Ass. 30, by the latter, support his statement. The report runs thus: "Alice *de W, qui fuit de l'age de xiij ans, fuit arse per judgment, pur ceo que el'avoit tue sa Maistres, & pur tant ceo fuit adjudge treason, &c.*;" and it appears that the case turned upon the question of accountability, by reason of the tender age of the culprit. No mention of drawing is made in the judgment. Compare H.P.C., i. p. 382, and note, with Hawk. P.C., b. 2, ch. 48, § 6, and authorities there referred to, and Coke, *ut supra.* Also, see 4 Black.

Comm. 204. It will have been noticed that though the judgment against Phillis was that she *go* to the place of execution, the warrant required that she be drawn thither. The practice of drawing, in such cases, would have been challenged, probably, if the cruelties anciently incident thereto had not become obsolete.

[10] Page 264.

[11] 2 Mass. Hist. Coll., vol. ii. p. 166, and note.

[12] See Hutchinson's Hist. Mass. Bay, vol. iii. p. 287, n. Instances of pardons and reprieves occur in our judicial history, but they were invariably granted in the name of the king, by the commander-in-chief; and, if for a graver offence than manslaughter, it seems to have been understood that a pardon was not to be granted without previous express direction from the king. This was in compliance with a clause in the royal instructions, issued to all the governors, by which they were enjoined not to remit any fines or forfeitures above £10 in amount, or to dispose of escheats, without the royal sanction; forfeiture of lands and chattels being a consequence of attainder upon conviction of the higher class of felonies. The commission to Andros expressly excepted treason and murder from the offences which he was authorized to pardon.

[13] Hist. Coll. Essex Inst., vol. xviii. p. 88, n.

[14] Letter of Colonel Revere to Cor. Sec. of Mass. Hist. Soc., Jan. 1, 1798: 1 Mass. Hist. Coll., vol. v. p. 107.

[15] Although the record contains no allegation of loss of life, Increase Mather states in his diary, under date of Sept. 22, 1681, that a child was burnt to death in one of the houses set on fire by this negress. Even if this were true, it is not probable that the relation of master and servant subsisted between the deceased and Maria, and neither this relation, nor the fact of treason, is averred in the indictment. See Mass. Hist. Soc. Proc., vol. iii. p. 320.

[16] Boston, Sept. 6, 1681.

[17] I have followed Secretary Rawson in his peculiar use of the letter j. See many similar instances in the Mass. Colony Records.

[18] Mass. Colony Laws, ed. 1672, p. 52.

[19] Exodus xxi. 25. "In all criminall offences, where the law hath prescribed no certaine penaltie, the judges have power to inflict penalties, according to the rule of God's word."—Declaration of the General Court: Hutch. Coll. Papers, p. 207. And see the first article of the Colonial "Liberties," in Mass. Hist. Coll., vol. viii. p. 216.

[20] Records of the Court of Assistants, 1674, p. 14.

[21] By the stat. 8 Hen. VI. ch. 6, the burning of houses, after a threat to do so if money be not paid, &c., was made high treason, and the incendiary suffered as any other traitor; that is, if a woman, she was burned to death. But this statute was repealed in the reign of Edward VI., as regards the treason, and the offence remained felony as at the common law, and punishable by hanging only.

That mistaken notions as to the nature of penalties to be inflicted in criminal cases, and as to the authority of the bench to impose unusual punishments, were not solely entertained in this distant colony, and among men not bred to the law, may be shown by many instances in the English law-books. One of the most notable is Sir Edw. Coke's reference to the case of Peter Burchet, a prisoner in the Tower,—who slew his keeper with a billet of wood, which drew blood,—as an authority for inflicting the additional punishment of cutting off the hand (under the stat. 33 Hen. VIII.) in the case of murder perpetrated in the king's palace, when attended with bloodshed. In Elderton's case, Chief Justice Holt, whose habits of thorough research were not less remarkable than his absolute fairness and honesty, said, "I have searched for the case cited [as Jones's case] about killing a man in the Tower. It is Burdelt and Muskett's case. Being dissatisfied with my Lord Coke's report of it, therefore I sent for the record, ... and there is judgment of death given, but no judgment that his right hand should be cut off. It is indeed so related in Stowe's Chronicle, and in fact his hand was cut off, but there was no judgment for it." Compare 3 Inst., ch. 65 (p. 140†) with 2 Ld. Raym., 978, 982.

[22] Record of the Court of Assistants, *ubi supra*, pp. 138, 139.

[23] *Ibid.*

[24] Deut. xxi. 22, 23.

[25] The ordinary punishment for all capital felonies during the colonial régime seems to have been simply hanging. Heretics and witches were subjected to no severer penalty; and in 1674, Robert Driver, who was convicted of murdering his master, Robert Williams of Piscataqua, and who thus incurred the penalty for petit treason, was sentenced to be "hanged by the neck until he be dead."—See Records of the Court of Assistants.

[26] 1 Mass. Hist. Coll., vol. iii. p. 152.

[27] *Ibid.*, 2d series, vol. ii. p. 102.

[28] Compare provincial statute 1750-51, ch. 17 (Prov. Laws, vol. iii. p. 540), with the act of parliament referred to.

[29] See a picture of the new gallows, in the illustrated "Newgate Calendar."

[30] The Massachusetts act is as follows:—

"Whereas it does not appear reasonable any longer to continue the distinction between the crimes of murder and petit treason:

"Be it enacted by the Senate and House of Representatives, in General Court assembled, and by the authority of the same, That from and after the passing of this act, in all cases wherein heretofore any person or persons would have been deemed or taken to have committed the crime of petit treason, such person or persons shall be deemed and taken to have committed the crime of murder only, and indicted and prosecuted to final judgment accordingly; and the same punishment only shall be inflicted as in the case of murder.—[This act passed *March 16, 1785*.]"

[31] Compare act of June 30, 1784, with Prov. Stat. 1728-29, ch. 15: Prov. Laws, vol. ii. p. 516.

Milton Keynes UK
Ingram Content Group UK Ltd.
UKHW030743071024
449371UK00006B/583